EARTH'S LANDFORMS

HILLS

by Lisa J. Amstutz

Raintree is an imprint of Capstone Global Library Limited, a company incorporated in England and Wales having its registered office at 264 Banbury Road, Oxford, OX2 7DY – Registered company number: 6695582

www.raintree.co.uk
myorders@raintree.co.uk

Edited by Alesha Sullivan
Designed by Bobbie Nuytten
Original illustrations © Capstone Global Library Limited 2021
Picture research by Kelly Garvin
Production by Tori Abraham
Originated by Capstone Global Library Ltd

978 1 3982 0276 4 (hardback)
978 1 3982 0275 7 (paperback)

British Library Cataloguing in Publication Data
A full catalogue record for this book is available from the British Library.

Acknowledgements
We would like to thank the following for permission to reproduce photographs: Alamy/MedSci, 11 ; Capstone Press/Karon Dubke, 20; Dreamstime: Helen Hotson, 15, Timothy Epp, 13 (top); Shutterstock: bdavid32, cover, Eric Poulin, 17 (bottom), Gerry Bishop, 10, Kevin Eaves, back cover, Mikhail Semenov, 9, Pelikh Alexey, 6, S Quintans, 13 (bottom), Sean Pavone, 19, Simun Ascic, 7, Steve Oehlenschlager, 17 (top), Zoom Team, 5

Printed and bound in India

Contents

Words in **bold** are in the glossary.

WHAT IS A HILL?

Have you ever run up a hill? A hill is a type of **landform**. It is higher than the land around it. But it is not as tall as a mountain. A hill can be big or small.

The top of a hill is called a peak. It can be pointed or flat. The sides of a hill can be high and **steep**. Others are low with sides that are less steep. Trees or grass cover some hills. Others are rocky and dry.

HOW ARE HILLS MADE?

Hills form in different ways. Underground there are big rocky plates. These plates move on top of melted rock in Earth's **crust**. The plates can bump into each other. They push up the land above them. It makes a hill.

Wind and water can make hills too. They wear away mountain peaks. Over time, the mountain gets smaller. Then it is a hill.

Some hills are made by sheets of ice. They wash away rock and soil as they melt. They leave piles of rock and soil behind.

TYPES OF HILLS

There are many types of hills. A pingo is made of land on top of ice. It forms in cold places. The ice never melts.

A mesa has steep rocky sides. It has a large flat top. Mesas are found in **deserts**.

pingo

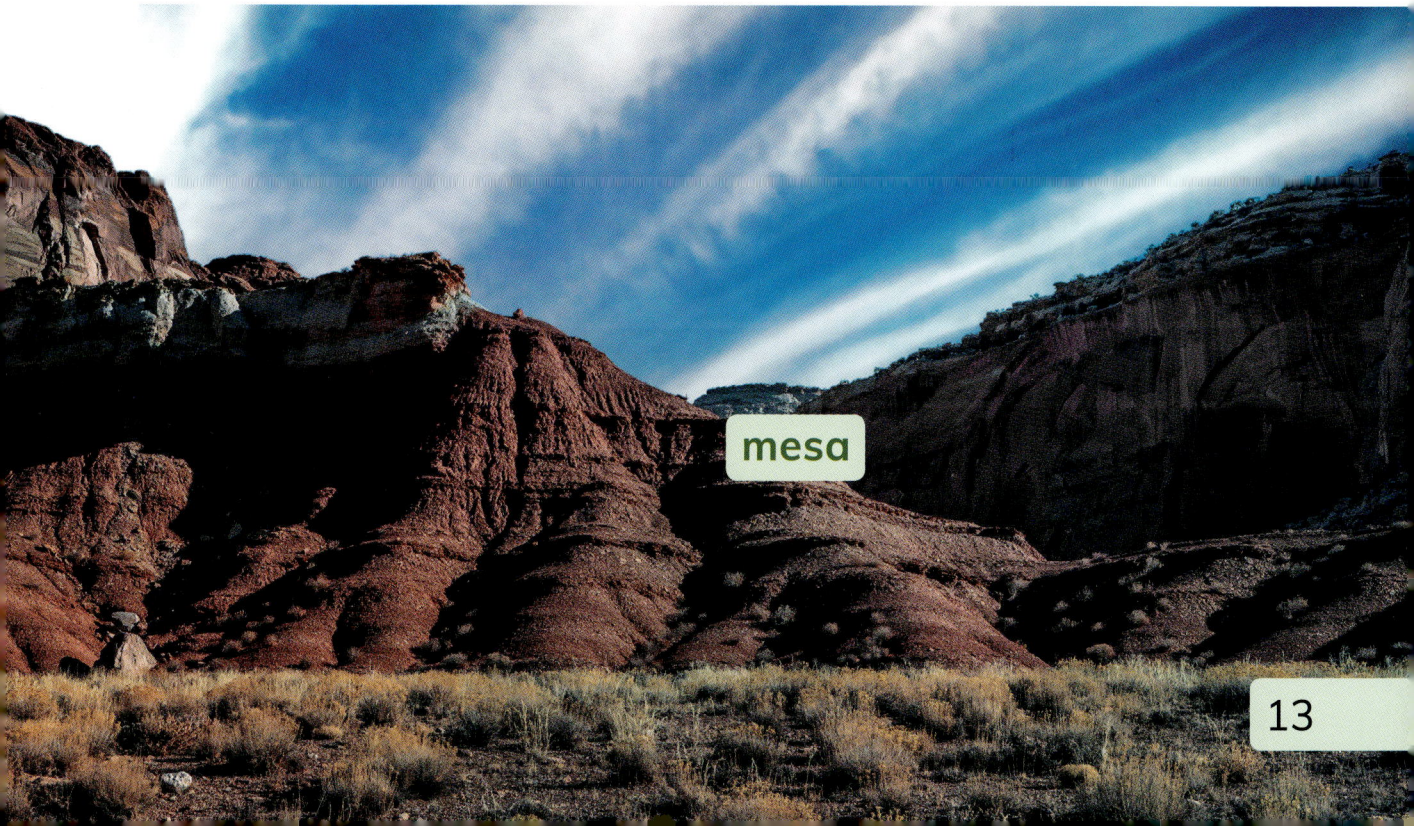

mesa

WHERE ARE HILLS FOUND?

Hills can be found all over the world. Some hills stand alone. Other hills are in groups. The Great Dyke is a group of hills in Africa. Many **minerals** are found in these hills. People look for gold and silver there.

WHAT LIVES ON A HILL?

Plants and animals live on hills. Trees, grass and bushes grow on some hills. Animals make homes there too. Foxes dig **burrows** in the ground. Birds make nests in trees. Snakes hide under rocks. Bighorn sheep climb the sides of steep hills.

Long ago, people lived on hills. On hills, people could see far. They stayed safe from **floods**. Many people still live on hills today. Would you like to live on a hill?

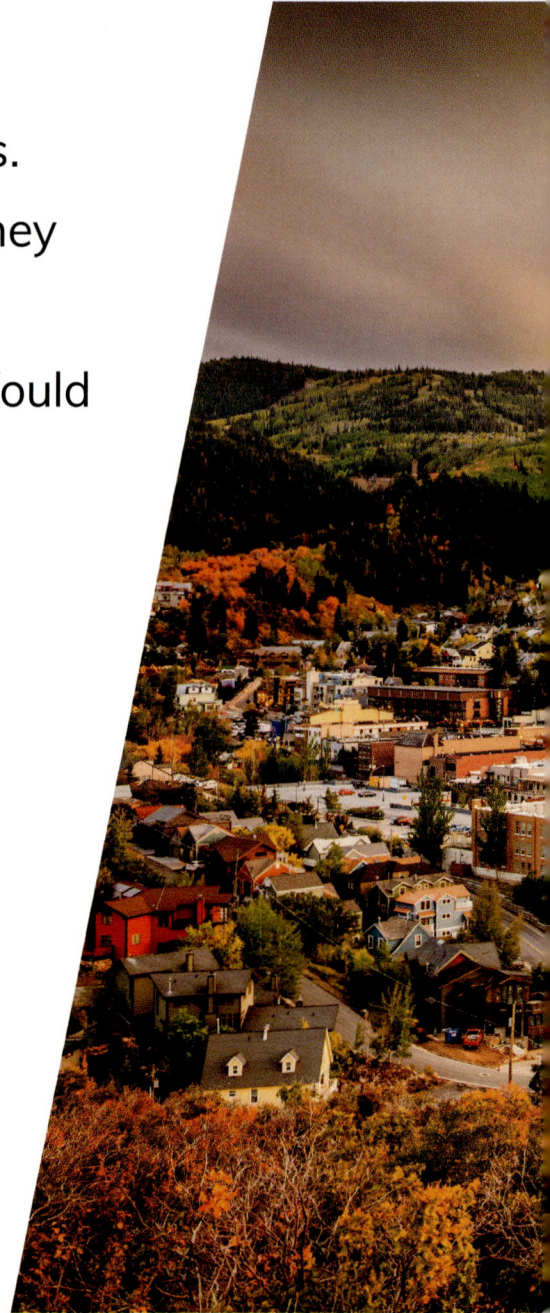

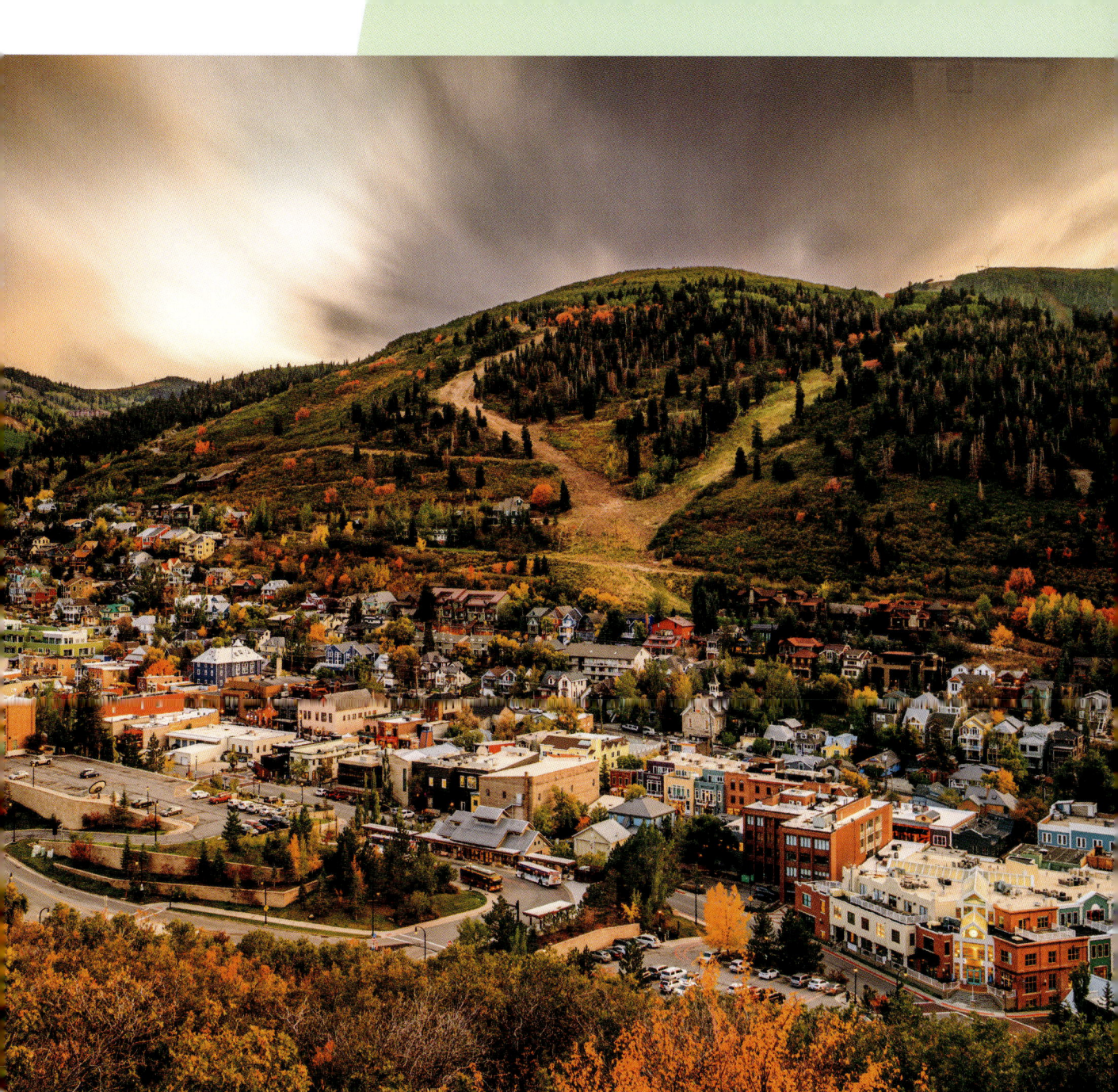

MAKE A HILL

Learn how wind and water can break down mountains to form hills.

You'll need:

- soil or compost
- container
- spray bottle filled with water
- straw

Instructions:

1. Pile up some soil in a container to make a mountain. Make sure the mountain has a pointy peak!

2. Use the straw to blow on your mountain. What happens to the soil? How does this "wind" affect the mountain?

3. Spray the top of your mountain with water. Watch how the soil runs off. How does this "rain" affect the mountain?

Glossary

burrow hole in the ground made or used by an animal

crust hard outer layer of Earth

desert dry area with little rain

flood overflow of water beyond the normal limits

landform natural feature of the land

mineral material found in nature that is not an animal or a plant

steep having a sharp slope or slant

Find out more

Books

DKfindout! Earth, DK (DK Children, 2017)

Earth's Landforms (Earth By Numbers), Nancy Dickmann (Raintree, 2018)

My Book of Rocks and Minerals, Dr Devin Dennie (DK Children, 2017)

Websites

www.dkfindout.com/uk/history/iron-age/hill-forts
Find out how people used to use hills for protection.

www.dkfindout.com/uk/earth/structure-earth
Find out more about the structure of Earth.

Index